ANCIENT INDIAN SCHOLARS JOURNEYS OF THE WISE

SCIENCE IN HINDUISM

Ranjini Sridhar

Contents

Fossilised Vasuki Indicus

Vasuki the king of serpents (Nagas) play a significant role in in the Matsya and Kurma incarnations of Lord Vishnu. Matsya uses Vasuki during Mahapralaya which high lights the cyclical nature of creation, preservation and dissolution. Vasuki wraps around Mount Mandara while churning the rod during Samudra Mantana in Kurmavatara signifies cooperation between opposing forces to achieve a common goal.

In contemporary times, Professor Sunil Bajpai and Debjit Datta from IIT Roorkee made a significant discovery of the fossilized Vasuki indicus. They discovered enormous fossils of Vasuki Indicus in Kutch, Gujarat in 2005 which was 10 to 15 metres in length. Vasuki Indicus belonged to the extinct relic lineage and was present in the middle Eocene period about 47 million years ago. The researchers say that Vasuki indicus might have been the size of a Titanoboa which was 50 ft in length and 3ft wide.

These parallels and distinctions create a fascinating intersection between mythological narratives and scientific discoveries.

Acharya Veda Vyasa

Based on various sources Acharya Veda Vyasa's period could be placed possibly around 3000 BCE – 2800 BCE, though these dates are debated.

Acharya Veda Vyasa is credited with several monumental compilations and compositions that have had a lasting impact on Hindu literature, philosophy, and culture as given here under:

1. Compiling and categorising the Vedas into four distinct texts:

- **Rigveda**
- **Samaveda**
- **Yajurveda**
- **Atharvaveda**

2. Mahabharata

3. Bhagavad Gita

4. Puranas: Vyasa is credited with composing eighteen Puranas, which are Brahma Purana, Padma Purana, Vishnu Purana, Shiva Purana, Bhagavata Purana, Narada Purana, Markandeya Purana, Agni Purana, Bhavishya Purana, Brahmavaivarta Purana, Linga Purana, Varaha Purana, Skanda Purana, Vamana Purana, Kurma Purana, Matsya Purana, Garuda Purana and Brahmaanda Purana.

5. Brahma Sutras (Vedanta Sutras): These aphoristic texts systematize and summarize the philosophical teachings of the Upanishads. The Brahma Sutras are one of the foundational texts of Vedanta philosophy.

6. Other Compliations: Harivamsa, An appendix to the Mahabharata, focusing on the life of Krishna and Adhyatma Ramayana, A spiritual rendition of the Ramayana attributed to Vyasa.

Acharya Veda Vyasa's work represents a synthesis of diverse spiritual and philosophical traditions of ancient India. His works continue to be studied, revered, and followed by millions around the world.

Agasthya Samhita

सस्थाप्य मृण्मये पत्रे ताम्रपत्रम् सुसंस्कृतम्. छाद्येच्छिखिग्रीवेन छर्दर्भिः कष्टपांसुभिः दस्तालोष्टो निधातव्यः पर्दच्छादितस्तः सन्नोगज्जायते तेजो मित्रवरुण सङ्गिग्यतम्

Take an earthen pot, place a copper plate and add the neck of a peacock which means copper sulphate. Then add wet saw dust and Zinc Amalgum. Contact with Mitra Varuna produces light. Mitra is cathode and Varuna is anode.

When a cell was formed using this method and measured with a digital multimeter, it had an open Circuit voltage of 1.38 volts and short circuit current of 23 milli amperes.

यवक्षारम्यौद्धनौ मृणालौ धात्वा यथाक्रमं। विनिर्माणे प्रकृतिस्थे समुद्धृत्य निवेशयेत्॥

"In the manufacturing process, after preparing tin and lead with alkali, it is important to mix them carefully."

This verse appears to describe a step-by-step process in metallurgy, specifically mentioning the preparation and mixing of tin (yava) and lead (audhana) using an alkali substance (kṣaara).

Acharya Agasthya

Acharya Agasthya is one of the Maharishis. He lived in the Rigvedic period (1950BC-1100). He was the Kula guru of King Dasharatha.

Agasthya Samhita is attributed to Acharya Agasthya. Agasthya Samhita contains a wealth of knowledge on various scientific topics, including the composition for making electric batteries. Agasthya Samhita also mentions that water can be split into oxygen and hydrogen.

He has written several texts on various chemical processes related to the preparation of medicines and metallurgy.

Acharya Agasthya also developed advanced irrigation techniques. These techniques ensured a continuous supply of water to the agricultural fields.

Agasthya's work in hydraulic engineering reflects the advanced state of technical and scientific knowledge in ancient India. He integrated engineering with sustainability.

References to Acharya Agasthya in the Vedas highlight the importance and respect he has gained for his knowledge and contribution.

Aryabhatia

चतुर्गुणितं तद्वर्गं राशिगुणितं सागरसंवृत्तम्। समस्तस्यासत्रं व्यासार्धं व्यासो हि यावत्॥

The geometric interpretation of the shloka is area of the circle is equal to half the circumference multiplied by half the diameter.

कलाक्रमेण योज्येत करणीयं भानौ ज्या। तत्कालयन्ति यत्रोदयस्थस्यागच्छतोः॥

"When calculating time, one should consider the sine of the arc. This represents the time it takes for the sun to move from sunrise to its current position."

Acharya Aryabhata

Acharya Aryabhata was an Indian mathematician and astronomer. He lived between 476 CE and 550 CE. Acharya Aryabhatta wrote "Aryabhatiya" when he was 23 years old. "Aryabhatiya" is a concise yet comprehensive treatise that covers various aspects of mathematics and astronomy.

Acharya Aryabhata's Aryabhatiya is divided into four divisions as follows:

- Gitakapada: Discusses large units of time, including the Yugas.

- Ganitapada: Covers arithmetic, algebra, plane trigonometry and spherical trigonometry.

- Kalakriyapada: Deals with different units of time, calendrical calculations, and the movement of celestial bodies.

- Golapada: Describes the geometric and trigonometric principles related to astronomy.

His key contributions were:

- Place value system and zero.

- Approximation of pi to 3.1416.

- Introducing sine (jyaa) and cosine (kojyaa).

- Quadratic equations and solving them.

- Concept of Earth rotating on its axis.

- Explanation of lunar and solar eclipses.

- Accuracy in calculating sidereal periods of Earth and other planets.

Acharya Aryabhata's work laid the foundation for later advancements in these fields. India's first satellite, launched in 1975, was named after him in his honor.

Baudhayana Sulbhasutra

दीर्घस्याक्षणयारज्जुः पार्श्वमानी तिर्यग्मानी च यत्पृथग्भूते कुरुतस्तदुभयाङ्करोटीति।

"A rope extended along the diagonal creates an area formed by the vertical and horizontal sides."

This can be understood as a statement of the Pythagorean theorem.

चतुरधिकम् शतमानं रज्जुराष्ट गुणं द्वागुणं वर्धः। आसन्ने वज्रमुखे त्रिभ्यां वृत्तं निक्षिप्यति॥

"Add four times a hundred to eight times sixty. The diameter obtained is stretched by one third. By the perpendicular (chord) of the (flanks of the square) having made (a hole), a circle is (drawn)."

In ancient Indian mathematics, this method was used to estimate the value of pi as approximately 3.125.

Acharya Baudhayana

Acharya Baudhayana was the first mathematician to derive Pythagoras' theorem. He lived between 800 BC and 740 BC.

"Baudhayana Sulbhasutra" contains geometric rules such as the construction of triangles and squares. The word sulbha means "chord" or "rope", indicating ropes in geometric constructions. Baudhayana Sulabhasutra provided an early statement of the Pythagoras theorem.

Some of the Key geometrical principles attributed to Acharya Baudhayana are:

- Pythagoras Theorem
- Area of a Circle
- Geometric Constructions
- Algebraic Principles

These theorems were used in the practical context of constructing sacrificial altars, which required precise geometric calculations.

Acharya Baudhayana contributed to mathematics and geometry. Acharya Baudhayana's work laid the foundation for later developments in Indian mathematics.

Sidhhantha Shiromani (Bijaganita)

वर्गं वर्गसमीभूतं रूपं वा रूपिणः पुनः। यो राशिर्यो गुणो यत्र कार्यो भूमिर्हि कल्प्यते॥

"When a square is equal to another square or a number, or any number of forms are equated, the resulting quantity is the root that should be considered for calculations."

This shloka encapsulates the essence of solving quadratic equations, which involve terms squared and equated to either other squares or numbers.

Acharya Bhaskaracharya II

Bhaskaracharya II was an Indian mathematician and an astronomer in the 12th century. He was born in 1114 CE in Bijapur Karnataka.

Bhaskaracharya II authored several important treatizes in mathematics and astronomy. Some of his notable texts include:

1. "Karana Kautukam": This is a detailed treatise that focuses on the construction and use of various astronomical instruments.

2. "Vasantotsava": This work delves into astronomy, specifically addressing the calculations related to planetary positions.

3. "Siddhanta Shiromani": This is a comprehensive treatise that covers various aspects of astronomy and mathematics.

"Siddhanta Shiromani" is divided into four parts as follows:

- Lilavati: A treatise on arithmetic, algebra, geometry, and mensuration. It covers a wide range of mathematical topics.

- Bijaganita: An algebraic treatise that deals with topics such as equations, surds, quadratic equations, and indeterminate equations. It is one of the most important works on algebra in Indian mathematics.

- Goladhyaya: A treatise on the celestial sphere, spherical astronomy, and related topics.

- Grahaganita: A treatise on planetary calculations

Bhaskaracharya was regarded for his astronomical and mathematical framework, which integrated observational data with mathematical theories. His deep understanding of both the theoretical and the practical aspects of astronomy in his time is remarkable.

Brahmasphutasiddhanta

व्यासार्धमेकं त्रयशद्धतं च युतं तदर्धं व्यासमितं च रूपम्। व्यासार्धवर्गेषु च फलकानि सिद्धं भविष्यत्त्रिभुजक्षेत्रम्॥

The diameter multiplied by three and then increased by ten percent is close to the circumference. The area of the circle is the product of the square of the radius and 3.

रिनं श्रिणं च यत्र, गुणना च वा विभाग: । रिनं रिणेऽस्ति लाभ:, श्रिणं श्रिणेऽस्ति वर्धनम् ॥

"Negative multiplied by negative is positive, and negative divided by negative is positive. Negative and positive multiplied by each other or divided by each other gives a negative result."

Acharya Brahmagupta

Acharya Brahmagupta, an Indian astronomer, and mathematician, lived from 598 CE to 668 CE. Acharya Brahmagupta made significant contributions to mathematics. At the age of 30, "Brahmasphutasiddhanta" and at the of 67 "Khandakhadyaka" were composed by Acharya Brahmagupta.

In 628 CE, Acharya Brahmagupta first described gravity as "Grutvakarshanam," an attractive force.

Some of the key highlights of Acharya Brahmagupta's contributions were:

- He was among the first to treat zero as a number and to define its mathematical operations.

- He formulated rules for dealing with positive and negative numbers and operations like addition, subtraction, multiplication, and division.

- He introduced methods for solving simultaneous and linear equations and some higher-degree equations.

- He gave the formula for the area of a cyclic quadrilateral.

- He enhanced the methods of accurate calculation of planetary positions and eclipses.

- He worked on improving the Indian calendar.

Brahmagupta became an astronomer of the Brahmapaksha school. Later, Brahmagupta moved to Ujjaini, Avanti, a major centre for astronomy in central India.

Acharya Brahmagupta's pioneering work with zero and negative numbers, his solutions to algebraic equations and his advancements in geometry and astronomy were influential in India, the Islamic world, and later in medieval Europe.

Kautilya Arthashastra

अहिंसा परमो धर्मः सर्वस्यापि दमः श्रुतम्। तस्माद् धर्मपरो राजा न हिंसात् प्रियम् अर्हति॥

"Non-violence is the highest virtue; restraint is the ultimate control, according to all scriptures.

Therefore, a king devoted to righteousness should never accept violence."

मूलं हि राजा धर्मस्य नयस्य च यशस्विनः तस्मात् सर्वस्ववस्थासु राजा कार्यः समीक्ष्यते

"The king is indeed the root of dharma (righteousness) and policy; therefore, the king must always be carefully observed in all circumstances."

सुखं प्रजानां हिते हितम्, राज्ञः सुखं हिंसा न प्रजानाम्। प्रीयं हिंसात् न राज्ञस्य, प्रीयं च प्रजानां हितम्॥

"The happiness of the king lies in the happiness of his subjects; the welfare of his subjects is his own welfare. What is not pleasing to himself should not be done by the king; what is pleasing to his subjects should be done."

Acharya Chanakya

Acharya Chanakya was an ancient Indian Philosopher, economist, jurist, and royal adviser. Acharya Chanakya is also called Acharya Kautilya. Acharya Chanakya lived during the 4th century BCE.

He was the key figure in the establishment of the Maurya Empire serving as the chief adviser to Chandragupta Maurya.

He is recognized for his contributions as a strategist and political theorist. "Kautilya Arthashastra" was authored by Acharya Chanakya. "Kautilya Arthashastra" remains as a significant work in the corpus of ancient Indian literature. It offers insights into governance and political strategy, which is relevant to current systems.

His ideas on governance, economics, and statecraft contribute to political theory and administration. Acharya Chanakya's contributions have had a profound and enduring influence on India's intellectual legacy. His reputation as one of the foremost strategists and thinkers in ancient history is cemented.

Charaka Samhita

सर्वे भवन्तु सुखिनः। सर्वे सन्तु निरामयाः। सर्वे भद्राणि पश्यन्तु। मा कश्चिद् दुःखभाग्भवेत्॥

"May everyone experience happiness, good health, auspiciousness, and freedom from suffering."

आत्मानं सततं विद्यादात्मनो जगतो हितम्। आत्मानं सर्वभूतेषु यो न हिंस्यात् प्रियं प्रिये॥

"Always recognize the Self; what is beneficial for oneself and for the world. Treat others as you would treat what is dear to you, do not harm others."

Acharya Charaka

Acharya Charaka is the father of Ayurveda. Acharya Charaka was an ancient physician who lived around the 2nd century CE. "Charaka Samhita" is attributed to Acharya Charaka. The "Agnivesha Tantra" is the foundational text upon which the "Charaka Samhita" was built.

Charaka Samhita provides a comprehensive guide to Ayurveda medicines, detailing the principles of diagnosis, treatment, and herbal remedies. It remains one of the influential texts in the field of Ayurveda.

Charaka Samhita is divided into eight sections or Angas:

- Sutra or General Principles
- Nidaana or Diagnosis
- Vimaana or Specific Features
- Shaarira or Anatomy and Physiology
- Indriya or Prognosis
- Chikitsa or Therapeutics
- Kalpa or Pharmacy
- Siddhi or Success in Treatment

Acharya Charaka stressed preventive medicine, proper diet, and hygiene. He has been the cornerstone of Ayurveda. He emphasized the importance of understanding the body constitution, Prakriti, and the balance between three doshas – Vata, Pitta, and Kapha.

Ayurveda fields are a holistic alternative medicine even today.

Vaisheshika Sutra

वेगः निमित्तविशेषात् कर्मणो जायते वेगः निमित्तापेक्षात् कर्मणो जायते नियतादि क्रिया आरब्धं हेतुर्वाग्संयोगविशेषविरोधि

Motion (vega) is produced from particular causes of action (karma).

Motion (vega) is dependent on specific causes of action (karma) and is determined by certain conditions (niyata, etc.).

The initiated action (arabdha) is caused by contact (saṃyoga) and is opposed by specific resistances (virodhi).

This shloka describes the relationship between motion (vega), action (karma), and the specific causes or conditions (nimitta) that produce and influence motion.

उत्क्षेपणं विक्षेपणं चाक्षेपणं प्रसारणं आकाशेषु विक्षेपः

This Shloka explains movements. Upward movement (utkshepa), downward movement (avakshepa), contraction (akṣepa), and expansion (prasaaraṇa) occur in space (aakaasha).

Acharya Kanaada

Acharya Kanaada is also known as Acharya Kashyapa. Acharya Kanaada was a philosopher who developed Vaisheshika philosophy. His presence is assumed to be around the 6th century BCE, although the exact dates are unknown.

Acharya Kanaada's major work "Vaisheshika Sutra" discusses metaphysics and atomic theory. Vaisheshika philosophy is known for its naturalistic approach.

Acharya Kanaada is best known for his atomic theory, which says that everything in the universe is composed of indivisible, indestructible particles called the "paramanus" or atoms. According to him, these atoms combine to form different substances and objects in the world. He developed atomic theory 2600 years ago.

Vaisheshika philosophy is characterized by its analysis of reality through the concept of "padarthas" or categories of existence. These are Dravya or Substance, Guna or Quality, Karma or action, Saamaanya or Generality, Vishesa or Particularity, Samavaaya or Inherence and Abhava or Absence

Kanaada's work is a milestone in classical Indian philosophy. His systematic characterization of reality and emphasis on atomism demonstrates the sophisticated level of philosophical inquiry in ancient India.

Vedanga Jyothisha

अयनं उत्तरं यान्तं सवत्सरमिहोच्यते। देवानां प्रियमायाति पुण्यकालं तदुच्यते॥

"When the sun moves northward (Uttarayana), it is known as the auspicious period. This time is dear to the gods and is considered highly meritorious."

This shloka underscores the importance of Uttarayana as a sacred time for performing rituals and ceremonies, believed to bring great benefits and divine favour.

तां याम्यां संक्रान्तिं चन्द्रमाः प्रतिपद्यते। याम्ये विषुवतो मासे पित्र्याणं भागमश्नुते॥

"The moon follows that southern course (Dakshinayana) and, in the month of the southern solstice, attains the realm of the ancestors."

This shloka highlights the significance of Dakshinayana, particularly the transition marking the southern course of the sun, which is associated with the pitṛyāṇa, the path leading to the ancestors.

विचित्राणि नक्षत्राणि तदन्ये चन्द्रमाः तथा। भान्ति सूर्यस्य रश्मिभिः सर्वं हि परिबृंहते॥

"The various constellations and the moon shine brightly; all are enveloped by the rays of the sun".

This shloka emphasizes the central role of the sun in the Vedic understanding of astronomy, highlighting its influence on all celestial bodies.

Acharya Lagadha

The exact dates of Acharya Lagadha's life are not definitively known, but he is traditionally believed to have lived around the late Vedic period around 1200 to 800 BCE.

Lagadha's work, particularly the Vedanga Jyotisha, reflects the sophisticated level of astronomical and calendrical knowledge that was developed during this time.

Vedanga Jyotisha

The Vedanga Jyotisha is divided into two variants, the Rigveda Jyotisha and the Yajurveda Jyotisha. Both versions provide guidelines for calculating the positions of the sun and the moon, determining lunar months, and understanding the movements of constellations.

Here are some key concepts from Vedanga Jyotisha attributed to Acharya Lagadha:

- Nakshatra (Constellations): The text describes the 27 nakshatras and their significance in the lunar calendar.

- Tithi (Lunar Days): Detailed explanations of tithis, their importance, and how they are used to determine auspicious times for rituals.

- Kala (Time): Methods for measuring time, including divisions such as muhurtas (48-minute intervals), and their relevance to daily activities and rituals.

- Ritus (Seasons): The understanding of the six seasons in the Vedic calendar and their impact on agricultural and ritual practices.

- Sankranti (Solar Transitions): The movement of the sun through the zodiac signs and its effect on the seasons.

Rasaratnakara

रसो हि शौल्यं भजते ग्रहासुरान् शोषयति त्वग्विवृतासु सर्वतः। गात्रेषु गन्धं विकृतिं विनाशयेत् सर्वामयोपद्रवशान्तिकारकः॥

This shloka highlights the therapeutic properties of mercury as described in "Rasaratnakara."

रसो युक्तः सुचिः स्निग्धः सुपक्कः स च शुद्ध्येत्। रसेन पुटितो लोहो जीवत्येव न संशयः॥

This shloka emphasizes the importance of purification and the correct combination of substances in alchemical processes.

कज्जलीकरणं रासेः सर्वधातुविषोपमम्। तद्धि धातुविनिर्मुक्तं मृतं जीवयते ध्रुवम्॥

This shloka describes the preparation of 'kajjali,' a crucial compound in Indian alchemy made by combining mercury with sulfur. The process of making kajjali is considered a powerful detoxification method for metals.

Acharya Nagarjuna

Acharya Nagarjuna attributed to the 8th or 9th century. He was an Indian scientist and alchemist. He is often associated with significant contributions to the fields of chemistry and metallurgy.

"Rasaratnakara" is a famous text on Indian alchemy (Rasa Shastra). "Rasaratnakara" is attributed to Acharya Nagarjuna. The text discusses various aspects of alchemy. It includes preparation of medicines, purification techniques, and metallurgy. It is worth noting that "Rasaratnakara" explains the preparation of mercury and the transformation of metals.

Nagarjuna through his experiments discovered the conversion of gold-like substances through base metals. This technology is used by the jewelry industry for making artificial jewelry.

His approach of combined practical laboratory work with theoretical knowledge, reflects the bridging of ancient traditions with emerging scientific practices.

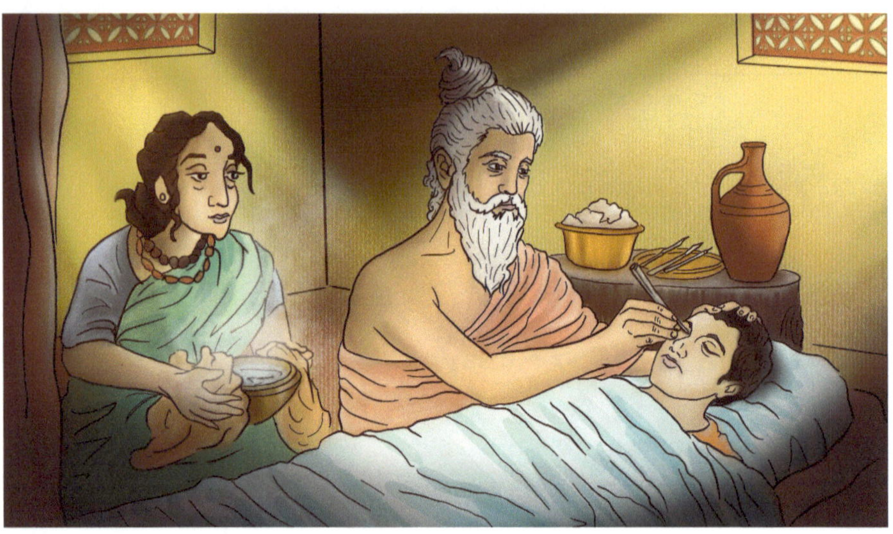

Sushruta Samhita

शरीरेन्द्रियसत्त्वात्मसंयोगो धर्मसंग्रहः। धृतिर्धर्मार्थकामानां स्वास्थ्यं मूलं ततः स्मृतम्॥

This shloka emphasizes the importance of skillful surgical intervention in wound management.

यत्नाद्धि शस्त्रदानेन कार्यः शल्यविनिर्ग्रहः। अन्यथा ह्यपसृष्टं स्यात् ततः क्लेशोऽधिकः स्मृतः॥

This shloka underscores the importance of careful and precise surgical technique, especially in the removal of foreign bodies.

Acharya Sushruta

Acharya Sushruta was a physician dated around the 6th Century BCE. He is known as the father of surgery. He authored the "Sushruta Samhita", an ancient Indian text on medicine and surgery describing surgical techniques and procedures. This comprehensive work covers various aspects of medicine including surgery, pharmacology, pathology, anatomy, and midwifery.

Key contributions of "Sushruta Samhita" include:

- Surgical techniques: The Sushruta Samhita includes nasal reconstruction, cataract surgery, removal of kidney stones along with various types of operations and suturing techniques. It is one of the earliest works to describe plastic surgery.

- Anatomical Knowledge: Includes a detailed description of the structure of the human body for successful surgery.

- Emphasis on Training and Ethics: Acharya Sushruta emphasized the importance of proper training for surgeons, highlighting the need for competence, hygiene, and compassion.

- Holistic Approach: His approach to medicine was holistic, integrating surgery with other aspects of health care, such as diet, exercise, and medicine.

The Sushruta Samhita remains significant in the history of medicine. "Sushruta Samhita" was translated into several languages over centuries and influenced medical practices in ancient Persia, Arabia, and Greece. "Sushruta Samhita" highlights the rich heritage of Indian medical knowledge.

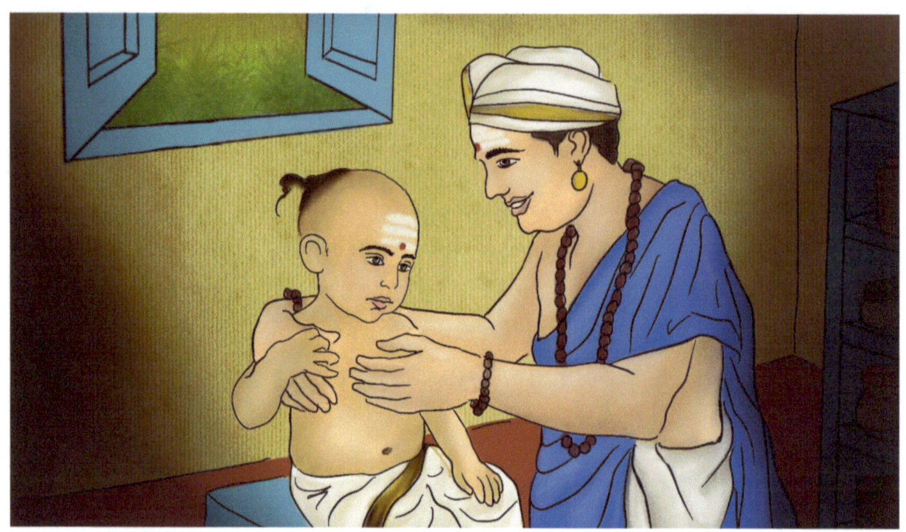

Kaumarabhritya

जाते स्नानं मृदितं त्वग्दोषानुत्सारणं च यत्। करिष्येत स्त्रीजनाः स्निग्धा बाहुप्रक्षेपणं च तत्॥

Upon birth, the newborn should be bathed and massaged with oil to remove impurities from the skin. This should be done by women with tender care, ensuring the baby is wrapped warmly.

मासानां त्र्याद्द्वि केचिद्ददति दशमात्परं। दन्तानां तु कफावृत्तौ खादयेन्न तु शिशुकम्॥

After six months or up to a year, supplementary feeding may be introduced, especially when the teeth begin to appear. However, care should be taken to avoid overfeeding the child.

श्लेष्माणं शिशवः सर्वे दोषं यान्ति यथासुखम्। ततः कासं श्वासमेव सजीर्णे चातिसारकम्॥

Children are prone to diseases caused by an imbalance of Kapha (mucus). This can lead to conditions like cough, asthma, and diarrhoea if digestion is impaired.

Acharya Vagabhatta

Acharya Vagabhatta was a renowned Ayurveda physician who lived around 7th century CE though the exact dates are uncertain.

He is credited with composing two major texts: the "Ashtanga Hridaya" and the "Ashtanga Sangraha." He synthesized and organized the knowledge from earlier Ayurvedic scholars like Charaka and Sushruta, making it more accessible and systematic.

Ashtanga Hridaya: The "Ashtanga Hridaya" (Heart of Medicine) is one of the primary texts authored by Acharya Vagabhatta. It is a concise, poetic compilation that simplifies and consolidates the vast amount of information found in earlier Ayurvedic texts. The text is divided into six sections or Sthaanas dealing with different aspects of medicine:

1. **Sutrasthana:** General principles of Ayurveda
2. **Sharirasthana:** Anatomy and physiology
3. **Nidanasthana:** Pathology
4. **Chikitsasthana:** Treatment
5. **Kalpasthana:** Toxicology
6. **Uttarasthana:** Specific therapies and additional topics

The "Ashtanga Hridaya" known for its clarity and systematic approach, makes it a core reference for Ayurvedic students and practitioners.

Ashtanga Sangraha: Acharya Vagabhatta provides detailed discussions on paediatric care in the "Ashtanga Sangraha".

Panchasiddhantika

ध्रुवाध्रुवं स्थितं भानुमपश्यन्ति सुरासुराः। ग्रहा अध्रुवं संस्थिताः स्म भुवनानि चरन्ति यत्र॥

This shloka describes the heliocentric model of the solar system, where the Sun (bhānum) is described as stationary (sthita) at the North Pole (dhruva). The planets (grahāḥ), however, are described as non-stationary (adhruvaṃ saṃsthitaḥ), moving (caranti) around the worlds (bhuvanāni), which refers to the Earth.

मंगलग्रहस्य कक्ष्या ज्ञेया व्योमविचक्षणैः। संख्यामुदग्रहितयां चतुर्थांशसमाः स्मृतः॥

This shloka provides a method for calculating the diameter of Mars based on observations. It states that the diameter of Mars (maṃgalagraha) is equal to four times the angular diameter (kakṣyā) observed during its opposition (udagrahita).

Brihat Samhita

वदन्ति केचित् तमसा ग्रस्तं राहुमुखेन च। चक्षुषोऽपि निमीलत्वान्न ग्रहणेऽस्ति भेदकः॥

In this shloka Varahamihira acknowledges a more scientific explanation, suggesting that the eclipse results from the alignment of celestial bodies, leading to the obstruction of the Sun's light.

Acharya Varahamihira

Acharya Varahamihira was an Indian astrologer, mathematician, and astronomer. He lived during the 6th century CE in Ujjain which was the renowned center for learning and astronomy in India. He served as one of the nine gems in the court of Vikramaditya.

Acharya Varahamira's "Panchasiddhantika" is a compilation of five earlier astronomical treatizes. It covers various aspects of mathematical astronomy including estimations on the diameters of planets like Mercury, Venus, Mars, Saturn, and Jupiter. It provides valuable insights into the celestial characteristics that created the structure of the solar system.

Acharya Varahamihira was the first to express how each planet in the solar system revolves around the Sun. His calculations of Mars' diameter were accurate within 11% of the currently accepted value. This precision of ancient Indian astronomical knowledge is remarkable.

Acharya Varahamihira's treatise on astrology, "Brihat Samhita", covers a wide range of subjects, including astrology, planetary movements, eclipses, rainfall, architecture, agriculture, and gemology.

Epilogue

To sum up, Science in Hinduism reflects a synthesis of empirical knowledge, metaphysical inquiry, and ethical considerations. It inspires curiosity and dialogue across disciplines contributing to a holistic understanding.

Key takeaways

Evolution

Parallels of Mass Extinction	Bhagavata Purana	3000 BCE – 2800 BCE

Medicine

Surgical Procedures	Sushruta Samhita	6th century BCE
Ayurveda Medicine	Charaka Samhita	2nd century CE
Paediatrics in Ayurveda	Kaumarabhritya	7th century CE

Astronomy

Seasonal changes, lunar and solar calendar	Vedanga Jyothisha	1200 BCE to 800 BCE
Planetary calculations	Siddhanta Shiromani	12th Century

Science

Innovation of electric batteries	Agasthya Samhita	1950 BCE – 1100 BCE
Laws of Motion	Vaisheshika Sutra	6th century BCE
Atomic Theory	Vaisheshika Sutra	6th century BCE
Architecture	Brihat Samhita	6th century CE
Indian Alchemy	Rasaratnakara	8th - 9th century CE

Mathematics

Pythagoras Theorem	Sulbhasutra	800 BCE – 740 BCE
Area of a Circle	Sulbhasutra	800 BCE – 740 BCE
Geometric Constructions	Sulbhasutra	800 BCE – 740 BCE
Place value system and zero.	Aryabhatia	476 CE – 550 CE
Approximation of pi to 3.1416.	Aryabhatia	476 CE – 550 CE
Introducing sine (jyaa) and cosine (kojyaa)	Aryabhatia	476 CE – 550 CE
Quadratic equations and solving them	Aryabhatia	476 CE – 550 CE
Concept of Earth rotating on its axis	Aryabhatia	476 CE – 550 CE
Explanation of lunar and solar eclipses	Aryabhatia	476 CE – 550 CE
Sidereal periods of Earth and other planets	Aryabhatia	476 CE – 550 CE
Zero as a number	Brahmasphutasiddhanta	598 CE – 668 CE
Positive and negative numbers	Brahmasphutasiddhanta	598 CE – 668 CE
Simultaneous and Linear equations	Brahmasphutasiddhanta	598 CE – 668 CE
Cyclic quadrilateral	Brahmasphutasiddhanta	598 CE – 668 CE
Mathematical topics	Lilavati	12th Century

Economics

Governance and Statecraft	Kautilya Arthashastra	4th century BCE